My First Music Book

Mi Primer Libro de Música

A Solfege, Recorder and Instrument Book
Un Libro de Solfeo, flauta dulce e Instrumentos

by Alfredo Aranda

Graphic Design: **Ana Laura Gallardo**
Diseño Gráfico:

Escuela de Música ™

Escuela de Música Publications

ISBN 1-932637-00-1 (Book/Libro)
ISBN 1-932637-01-X (CD Practice/ CD Práctica)
ISBN 1-932637-02-8 (CD Performance/ CD Presentaciones)
ISBN 1-932637-03-6 (DVD)

A

To my parents Guadalupe y Sara Aranda, for their unconditional support.

To my family... and specially to my niece Breana who showed me with her spontaneous way of caring, how to express my appreciation for all children through the lessons of this book.

Also I would like to thank all my teachers, students, colleagues and all who collaborated towards the making of this material.

They are too many that I can not mention them all by name, but... Thank you all!

A mis padres Guadalupe y Sara Aranda, por su incondicional apoyo en este proyecto.

A mi familia... y muy en especial a mi sobrina Breana quien con su espontánea demostración de cariño me ha motivado a expresar mi aprecio a todos los niños a través de las enseñanzas de este libro.

También quiero agradecer a todos mis maestros, alumnos, colegas y colaboradores que, sin sus aportaciones, hubiera sido imposible la realización de este material.

Son tantos que no los podría mencionar por nombre pero... ¡Gracias a todos!

Content by Theme
Contenido de Temas

	page página	
Redondita, Blanca, Voy	1	Redondita, Blanca, Voy
The Staff	2	El Pentagrama
The names of the notes	10	Los Nombres de las Notas
How to do the fingerings	12	Como se colocan los dedos en la flauta dulce
"Si" Third Line	13,14	"Si" Tercera Línea
"La" Second Space	15,16	"La" Segundo Espacio
"Sol" Second Line	17, 18	"Sol" Segunda Línea
"Re" Fourth Line	20, 21	"Re" Cuarta Línea
The Marcho and the Shh	23	El Marcho y el Shh
"Do" Third Space	24, 25	"Do" Tercer Espacio
"Re" Under the Staff	26, 27	"Re" Bajo el Pentagrama
The Blanquita and the Tie	29	La Blanquita y la Ligadura
Marcho, Marcho-Rest Note, Marcho-Note Rest	30	Marcho, Marcho-Silencio, Marcho-Figura y Silencio
"Mi" First Line	31, 32	"Mi" Primera Línea
Voy and Marcho Tied and its equivalent	34	Voy y Marcho Ligados y su equivalente
"Mi" Fourth Space	36, 37	"Mi" Cuarto Espacio
Fermata	39	El Calderón
"Fa Sharp" First Space	40, 41	"Fa Sostenido" Primer Espacio
Eighth Note	44	La Corchea
Vamonos & its variants	45	Vámonos y sus variantes
Beaming of the eighth notes	47	La Unión de las Corcheas
Repeat Signs	48	Signos de Repetición
Repeat signs ant its boxes	50	Signos de Repetición y sus Casillas
"Do Sharp" Third space	51,52	"Do Sostenido" Tercer Espacio
Marcho tied to a Voy & its equivalent	54	Marcho Ligado con Voy y su equivalente
"Si flat" Third Line	55, 56	"Si Bemol" Tercera Línea
"Fa" Fifth Line	57, 58	"Fa" Quinta Línea
"Fa" First Space	59, 60	"Fa" Primer espacio
"Do" First Line under the Staff	62, 63	"Do" Primera línea adicional bajo el pentagrama
The Ligerito & 2 marchos in Syncopated Rythm	65	El Ligerito y 2 marchos en Sincopa
"Sol Sharp" Second Line	66, 67	"Sol Sostenido" Segunda Línea
Ligerito-Galloping, Ligerito-Jumping	69	Ligerito-Galopa, ligerito-Saltillo
Ligerito, Double Jumping	71	Ligerito-Saltillo Doble
"Re Sharp" Fourth Line	75, 76	"Re Sostenido" Cuarta Línea
Ligerito-Galopa, Ligerito-Saltillo	78	Ligerito-Galopa, Ligerito-Saltillo
7 Aditional Lessons	83-89	7 Lecciones Adicionales
Low Register Fingering Chart	90	Digitación en Registro Bajo
High Register Fingering Chart	91	Digitación en Registro Alto

Content by Song
Contenido de Canciones

page
página

Songs	page	Canciones
Mary Had a Little Lamb	19	El Corderito De Maria
La Tía Nancy	22	La Tía Nancy
El Cucu	28	El Cucu
Amazing Grace, When The Saints Go Marching In	33	Abundante Gracia, La Marcha De Los Santos
Ode To Joy, Jingle Bells	35	Himno A La Alegría, Navidad
Are You Sleeping, Twinkle Twinkle Little Star	38	Martinillo, Estrellita
Happy Birthday, The Good Morning Song	42	Feliz Cumpleaños, Las Mañanitas
I Remember You, Michael Row Your Boat	43	Me Acuerdo De Ti, Miguelito Y Su Barquito
My Little Ranch, For He Is a Jolly Good Fellow	46	Mi Ranchito
Ding Dong Happiness Up High, Oh Come All Ye Faithful	49	Ding Dong Felicidad En Lo Alto, Venid Fieles Todos
Can-Can, Kum By Ya, Bridal Chorus	53	Can-Can, Kum By Ya, La Marcha Nupcial
Lullaby	61	Canción de Cuna
from "Winter"	64	de "Invierno"
from " The Nutcracker"	68	de "El Cascanueces"
Sailor, Beautiful Heaven	70	Marinero, Cielito Lindo
The Army, At The Park	72	El Ejercito, En El Parque
New Year, The Fair	73	Año Nuevo, En La Feria
Silent Night, Noel	74	Noche De Paz, Noel
from "Serenade", from "Swan Lake"	77	de "Serenata", de "El Lago De Los Cisnes"
from " Spring", Romance	79	de "Primavera", Romance
The Holly And The Ivy	80	El Acebo Y La Hiedra
The Good Morning Song	81	Las Mañanitas

"My First Music Book" is a book designed to give a beginning music student a solid foundation in the basic elements of rhythm, melody theory and practice. It contains a series of very popular melodies arranged in a way that introduces basic elements of rhythm, melody theory and recorder practice in the most gradual possible way. This book has helped thousands of children to quickly acquire the required skills to play and understand any musical instrument in a much faster way.

This book can be purchased alone or with the following materials that will greatly enhance the potential of learning it even with out the help of the teacher.

My First Music Theory book
Practice CD
Performance CD
Lessons on DVD

"Mi Primer Libro de Musica" es un libro diseñado para darle un firme fundamento a un principiante de musica en los elementos básicos de ritmo, melodía, teoría y practica del instrumento. Contiene una serie de canciones muy conocidas de todos los tiempos preparadas de tal manera que introducen elementos rítmicos, melódicos, teóricos junto con la practica de la flauta dulce de la manera mas gradual posible. Este libro a ayudado a miles de niños a que rápidamente adquieran los conocimientos y el sentido musical para tocar y entender cualquier instrumento.

Este libro puede ser comprado solo o con los siguientes materiales que aumentaran en gran manera su efectividad aun sin la ayuda de un maestro.

Mi Primer libro de Teoría Musical
CD de Practica
CD de Presentaciones
Clases en DVD

Four special icons accompany each song along with a faded circled check mark by them tell you the steps which should be taken to learn all songs contained in this book. Note all steps should be done very slowly for a few weeks even if the student thinks he (she) already knows the song.

Cuatro diferentes iconos acompañan cada canción junto con un circulo que dentro tiene una palomita gris. Esos iconos representan los pasos que debe hacer en cada canción. Note que todos los pasos son importantes y deben ser hechos de una manera lenta y repetirlos por algunas semanas auque el niño(a) ya se halla aprendido la canción.

The "Rhythm" icon tells you that the first step in learning the song is to clap the rhythmic symbols and say them at the same time. After this first step is completely mastered a check mark should be written on the side to measure your progress. This Icon may also tell you there is a new Rhythm symbol.

El icono de "Ritmo" nos dice que el primer paso para aprendernos la canción seria aplaudir el ritmo mientras decimos el nombre de la figura rítmica. Después que este paso halla sido dominado se podrá marcar la palomita para así poder medir el progreso del alumno. Este mismo icono también puede decirte que hay un nuevo ritmo.

The "Solfege" icon tells you that the second step in learning the song is to clap and say the names of the notes at the same time. After this second step is completely mastered a check mark should be written on the side to measure your progress.

El icono de "Solfeo" nos dice que el segundo paso para aprendernos la canción seria aplaudir el ritmo mientras decimos el nombre de las notas. Después que este paso halla sido dominado se podrá marcar la palomita para así poder medir el progreso del alumno.

The "Fingering" icon tells you that the third step in learning the song is to finger the recorder and say the notes at the same time. After this third step is completely mastered a check mark should be written on the side to measure your progress.

El icono de "Digitación" nos dice que el tercer paso para aprendernos la canción seria hace la digitación mientras decimos las notas con la boca. Después que este paso halla sido dominado se podrá marcar la palomita para así poder medir el progreso del alumno.

The "Play" Icon tells you that the fourth step in learning the song is to play the song. A brief explanation on how to blow into the recorder should be given before doing this step. After this fourth step is completely mastered a check mark should be written on the side to measure your progress.

El icono de "Tocar" nos dice que el cuarto paso para aprendernos la canción seria simplemente tocar la canción. Una breve explicación de como soplarle al instrumento debe ser dada antes de tocarlo. Después que este paso halla sido dominado se podrá marcar la palomita para así poder medir el progreso del alumno.

Additional icons through the book alert you to very important concepts.

Iconos adicionales dentro del libro nos alertan sobre conceptos importantes

The "Note icon" tells you that there is a new note to be learned

Icono de la "Nota". Nos dice que hay una nueva nota.

The "Hand icon" tells you to remember a recently new concept

Icono de la "Mano". Nos dice que recordemos un concepto recientemente aprendido

pum pum pum

Redondita	𝑜	= 4	*beats* tiempos
Blanca	𝅗𝅥	= 2	*beats* tiempos
Voy	♩	= 1	*beat* tiempo

Line / Línea 5			Space / Espacio 4
Line / Línea 4			Space / Espacio 3
Line / Línea 3			Space / Espacio 2
Line / Línea 2			Space / Espacio 1
Line / Línea 1			

How many LINES are there in the STAFF?
¿Cuántas LÍNEAS tiene el PENTAGRAMA? _____

How many SPACES are there in the STAFF?
¿Cuántos ESPACIOS tiene un PENTAGRAMA? _____

Write down the number of the lines and the spaces where they belong.
Escriba el número de las líneas y los espacios.

Line
Línea ——

Line
Línea ——

Line
Línea ——

Line
Línea ——

Line
Línea **1**

Space
Espacio ——

Space
Espacio **3** ——

Space
Espacio ——

Space
Espacio ——

How many LINES are there in the STAFF?
¿Cuántas LÍNEAS tiene el PENTAGRAMA?   _____

How many SPACES are there in the STAFF?
¿Cuántos ESPACIOS tiene un PENTAGRAMA?   _____

Where is the "Redondita"?
¿En dónde está la "Redondita"?

It is in line
Está en la línea _____

It is in line
Está en la línea _____

It is in line
Está en la línea _____

It is in line
Está en la línea _____

It is in space
Está en el espacio _____

It is in space
Está en el espacio _____

It is in space
Está en el espacio _____

It is in space
Está en el espacio _____

It is in line
Está en la línea _____

It is in space
Está en el espacio _____

It is in line
Está en la línea _____

It is in space
Está en el espacio _____

Line
Línea ___1___

Line
Línea ___2___

Line
Línea ___3___

Line
Línea ___4___

Space
Espacio ___1___

Space
Espacio ___2___

Space
Espacio ___3___

Space
Espacio ___4___

Line
Línea ___1___

Space
Espacio ___1___

Line
Línea ___2___

Space
Espacio ___2___

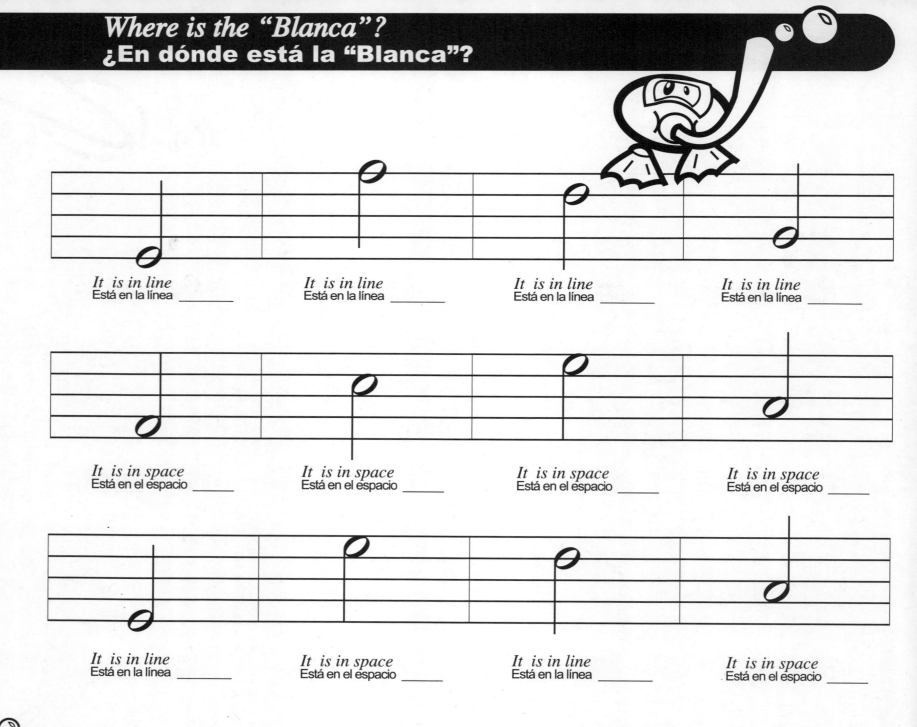

It is in line
Está en la línea _____

It is in line
Está en la línea _____

It is in line
Está en la línea _____

It is in line
Está en la línea _____

It is in space
Está en el espacio _____

It is in space
Está en el espacio _____

It is in space
Está en el espacio _____

It is in space
Está en el espacio _____

It is in line
Está en la línea _____

It is in space
Está en el espacio _____

It is in line
Está en la línea _____

It is in space
Está en el espacio _____

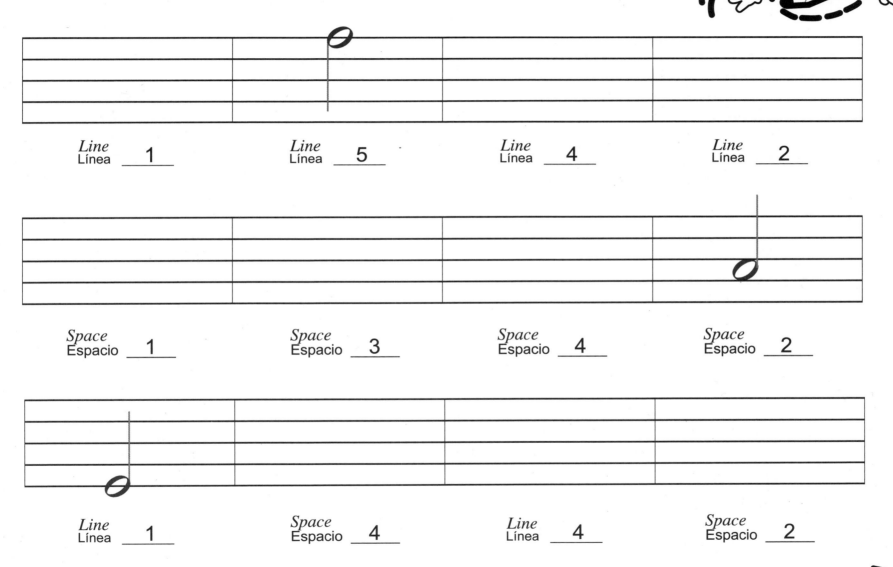

Line
Línea ___1___

Line
Línea ___5___

Line
Línea ___4___

Line
Línea ___2___

Space
Espacio ___1___

Space
Espacio ___3___

Space
Espacio ___4___

Space
Espacio ___2___

Line
Línea ___1___

Space
Espacio ___4___

Line
Línea ___4___

Space
Espacio ___2___

It is in line
Está en la línea _____

It is in line
Está en la línea _____

It is in line
Está en la línea _____

It is in line
Está en la línea _____

It is in space
Está en el espacio _____

It is in space
Está en el espacio _____

It is in space
Está en el espacio _____

It is in space
Está en el espacio _____

It is in line
Está en la línea _____

It is in space
Está en el espacio _____

It is in line
Está en la línea _____

It is in space
Está en el espacio _____

Line
Línea ___1___

Line
Línea ___2___

Line
Línea ___4___

Line
Línea ___5___

Space
Espacio ___3___

Space
Espacio ___2___

Space
Espacio ___1___

Space
Espacio ___4___

Line
Línea ___1___

Space
Espacio ___4___

Line
Línea ___4___

Space
Espacio ___2___

The names of the notes
Los nombres de las notas

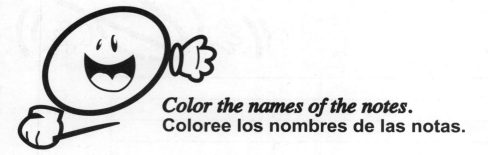

Color the names of the notes.
Coloree los nombres de las notas.

*Put your **Left Hand** in the space below; trace it with a pencil. Then put the numbers and the names of the finger on the tip of the finger. 1-thumb, 2-index, 3-third, 4-annular, 5-little.*

Coloque la **Mano Izquierda** en el espacio de abajo y dibújela con un lápiz. Después numere los dedos usando los numeros del 1 al 5 comenzando con el pulgar. Enseguida póngale los nombres a los dedos, 1-Pulgar, 2-índice, 3-medio 4-anular, y 5-meñique.

*Put your **Right Hand** in the space below; trace it with a pencil. Then put the numbers and the names of the fingers on the tip of the finger. 1-thumb, 2-index, 3-third, 4-annular,5-little.*

Coloque la **Mano Derecha** en el espacio de abajo y dibújela con un lápiz. Después numere los dedos usando los numeros del 1 al 5 comenzando con el pulgar. Enseguida póngale los nombres a los dedos, 1-Pulgar, 2-índice, 3-medio 4-anular, y 5-meñique.

Open
Abierto

Closed
Cerrado

1/3-1/4 Open
1/3-1/4 Abierto

Two inner circles opened
Dos círculos internos abiertos

One inner circle closed
Un círculo interno cerrado

Two inner circles closed
Dos círculos internos cerrados

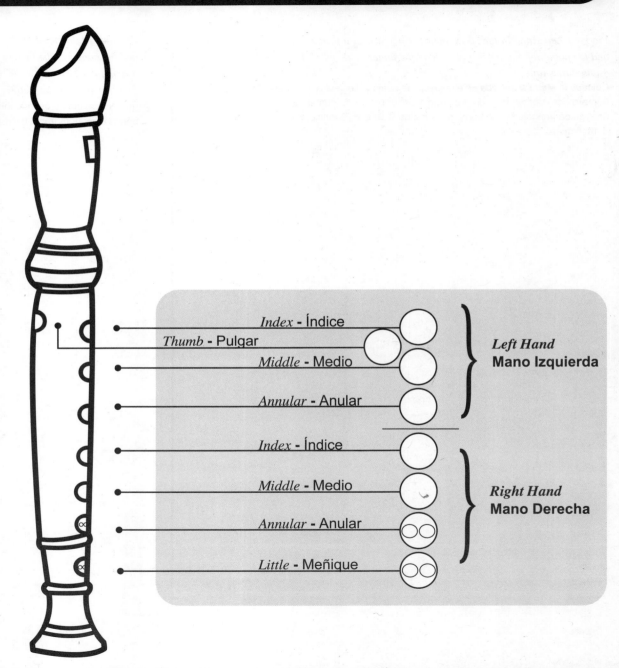

Index - Índice

Thumb - Pulgar

Middle - Medio

Annular - Anular

Left Hand
Mano Izquierda

Index - Índice

Middle - Medio

Annular - Anular

Little - Meñique

Right Hand
Mano Derecha

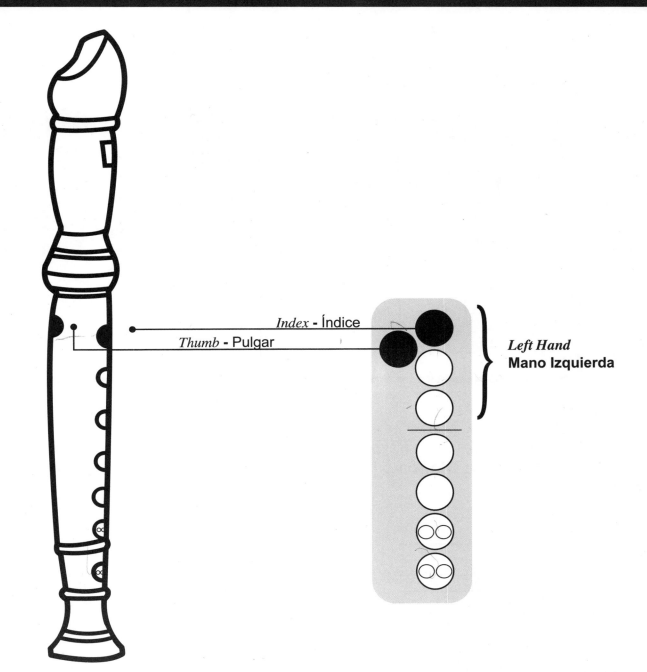

Index - Índice

Thumb - Pulgar

Left Hand
Mano Izquierda

Open
Abierto

Closed
Cerrado

"SI" Third line
"SI" Tercera línea

Color the "SI" note on the piano.
Coloree la nota "SI" en el piano.

*Every time the **Voy**, the **Blanca** or the **Redondita** is on the **Third Line** its name is:*
Cuando el **Voy**, la **Blanca** o la **Redondita** están en la **Línea 3** su nombre es:

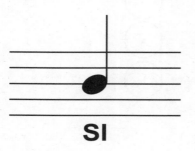

SI

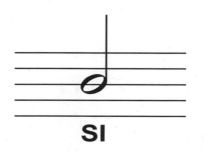

SI

SI

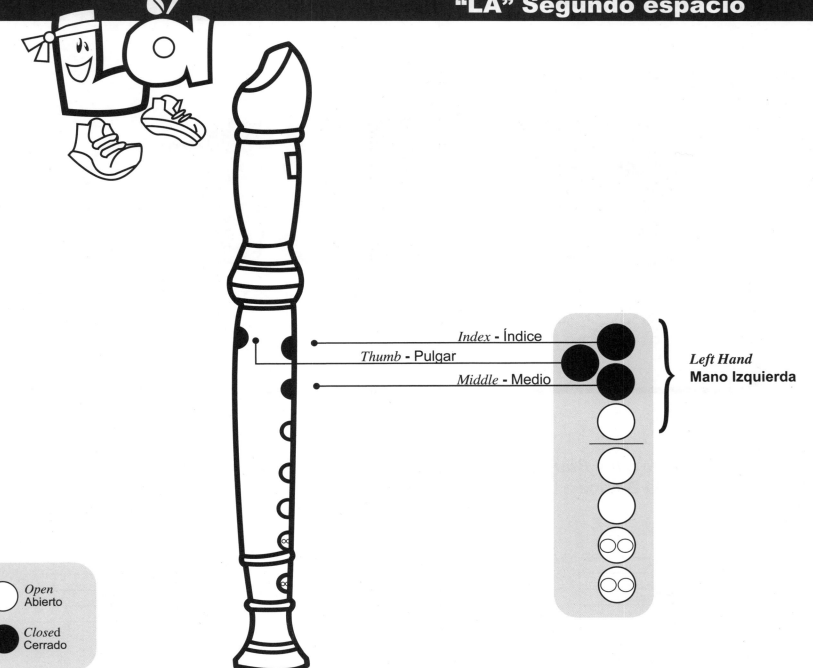

Index - Índice

Thumb - Pulgar

Middle - Medio

Left Hand
Mano Izquierda

Open
Abierto

Closed
Cerrado

"LA" Second space
"LA" Segundo espacio

Color the "LA" note on the piano.
Coloree la nota "LA" en el piano.

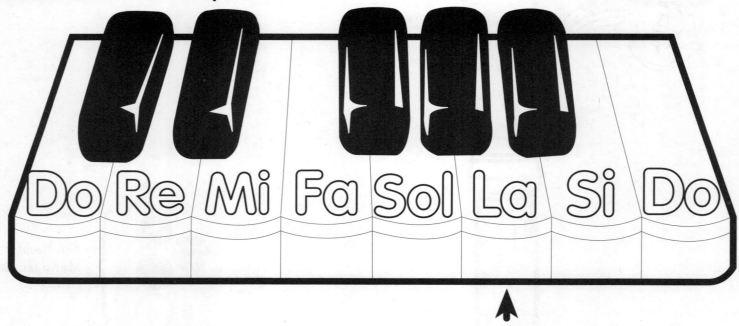

*Every time the **Voy,** the **Blanca** or the **Redondita** is on the **Second Space** its name is:*
Cuando el **Voy**, la **Blanca** o la **Redondita** están en la **Espacio 2** su nombre es:

LA

LA

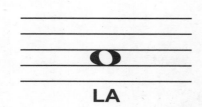

LA

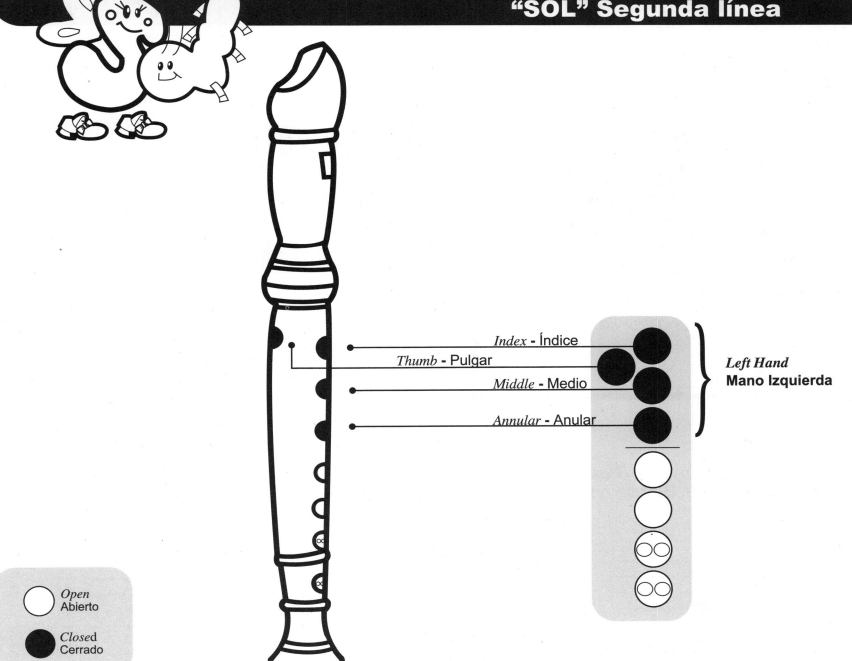

Index - Índice

Thumb - Pulgar

Middle - Medio

Annular - Anular

Left Hand
Mano Izquierda

Open
Abierto

Closed
Cerrado

Color the"SOL" note on the piano.
Coloree la nota "SOL" en el piano.

*Every time the **Voy,** the **Blanca** or the **Redondita** is on the **Second Line** its name is:*
Cuando el **Voy**, la **Blanca** o la **Redondita** están en la **Línea 2** su nombre es:

SOL

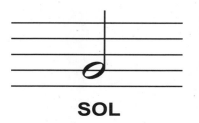

SOL

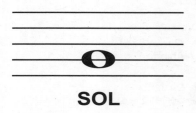

SOL

Note review.
Repaso de notas.

SI   LA   SOL

Mary had a little lamb
El corderito de María

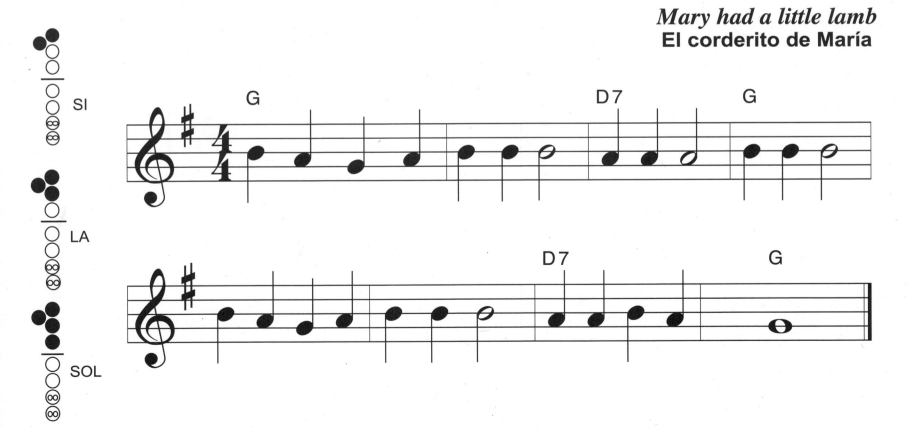

SI

LA

SOL

**High
Alto**

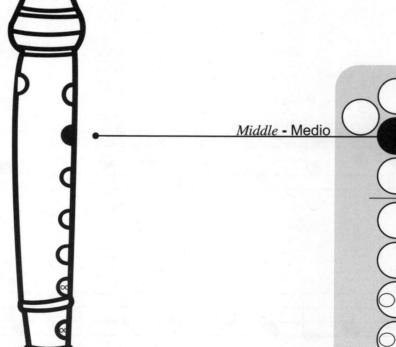

Middle - Medio

Left Hand
Mano Izquierda

○ *Open*
Abierto

● *Closed*
Cerrado

Color the "RE" note on the piano.
Coloree la nota "RE" en el piano.

*Every time the **Voy**, the **Blanca** or the **Marcho** is on the **Fourth Line** its name is:*
Cuando el **Voy**, la **Blanca** o el **Marcho** están en la **Línea 4** su nombre es:

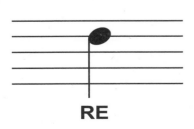

RE

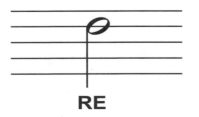

RE

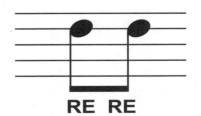

RE   RE

La Tía Nancy

Note review.
Repaso de notas.

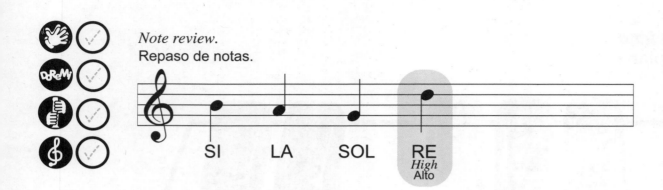

SI LA SOL RE *High* Alto

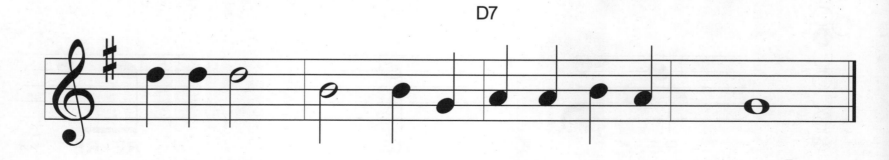

Marcho = **1** *beat* **tiempo**

Mar - cho

Shh  = **1** *beat* **tiempo**

Shh

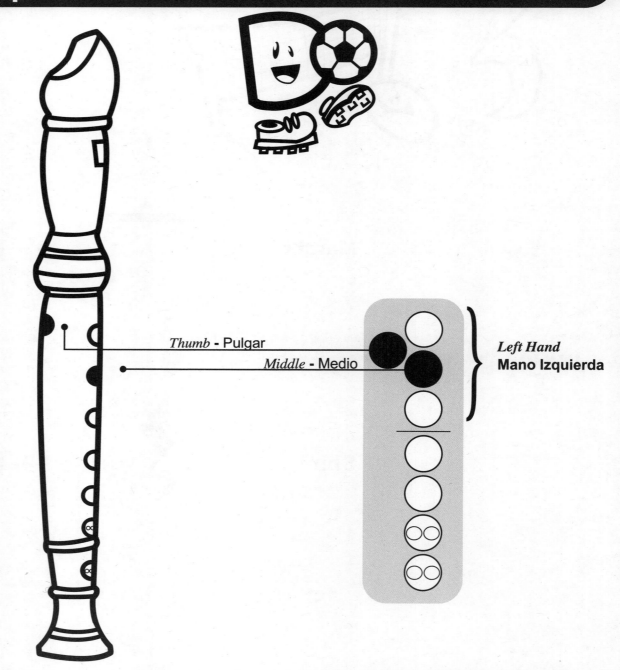

Thumb - Pulgar

Middle - Medio

Left Hand
Mano Izquierda

Open
Abierto

Closed
Cerrado

Color the"DO" note on the piano.
Coloree la nota "DO" en el piano.

*Every time the **Voy,** the **Blanca** or the **Marcho** is on the **Third Space** its name is:*
Cuando el **Voy**, la **Blanca** o el **Marcho** están en la **Espacio 3** su nombre es:

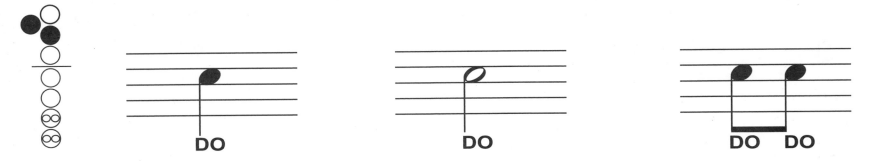

DO   DO   DO   DO

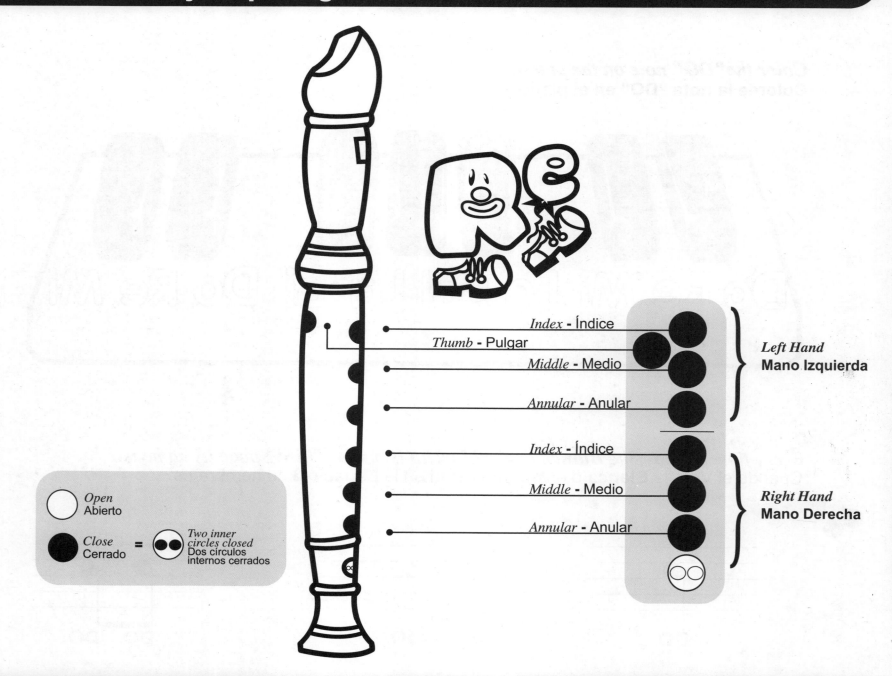

Index - Índice

Thumb - Pulgar

Middle - Medio

Annular - Anular

Left Hand
Mano Izquierda

Index - Índice

Middle - Medio

Annular - Anular

Right Hand
Mano Derecha

Open
Abierto

Close
Cerrado

= Two inner circles closed
Dos círculos internos cerrados

Color the"Low RE" note on the piano.
Coloree la nota "RE Bajo" en el piano.

Do Re Mi Fa Sol La Si Do Re Mi

*Every time the **Voy**, the **Blanca** or the **Marcho** is **Under the Staff** its name is:*
Cuando el **Voy**, la **Blanca** o el **Marcho** están **Bajo el Pentagrama** su nombre es:

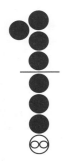

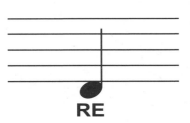

RE

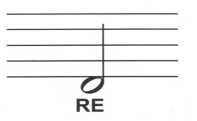

RE

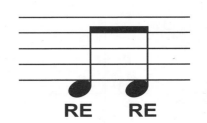

RE   **RE**

Note rewiew.
Repaso de notas.

SI LA SOL RE *High* Alto DO RE

El Cucú

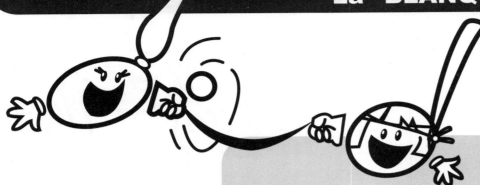

$\text{♩.} \quad = \quad 3 \quad \textit{beats} \quad \text{tiempos}$

Blanquita

$\text{♩.} \smile \text{♩} \quad = \quad 5 \quad \textit{beats} \quad \text{tiempos}$

Blanquita blanca

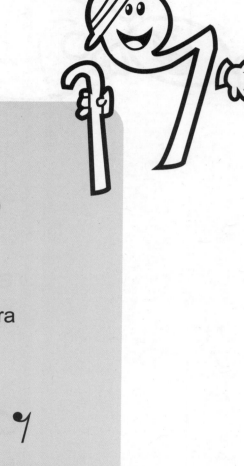

Mar - cho

Mar - cho
Rest - *Note*
Silencio - Figura

Mar - cho
Note - *Rest*
Figura - Silencio

Mar - cho   Mar - cho

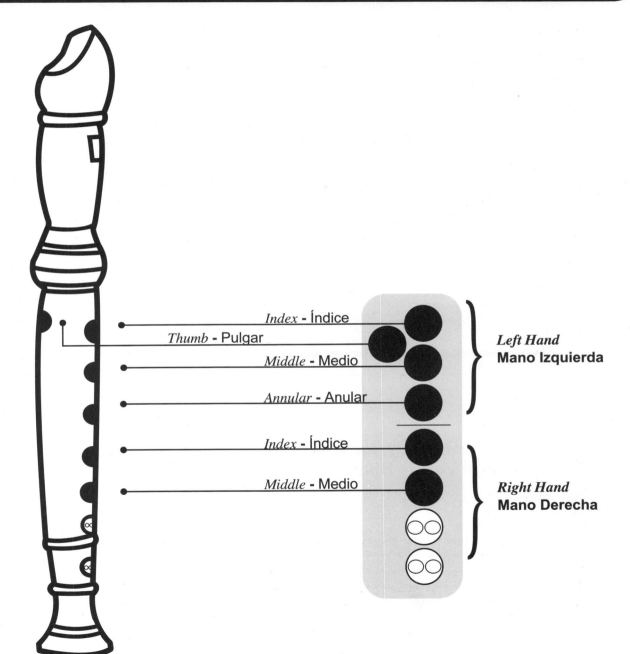

Index - Índice

Thumb - Pulgar

Middle - Medio

Left Hand
Mano Izquierda

Annular - Anular

Index - Índice

Middle - Medio

Right Hand
Mano Derecha

Open
Abierto

*Clos*ed
Cerrado

Color the "MI" note on the piano.
Coloree la nota "MI" en el piano.

*Every time the **Voy**, the **Blanca** or the **Marcho** is on the **First Line** its name is:*
Cuando el **Voy**, la **Blanca** o el **Marcho** están en la **Línea 1** su nombre es:

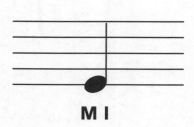

M I

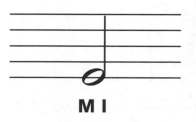

M I

M I   **M I**

Voy   Mar - cho   =   Voy   Mar - cho

High
Alto

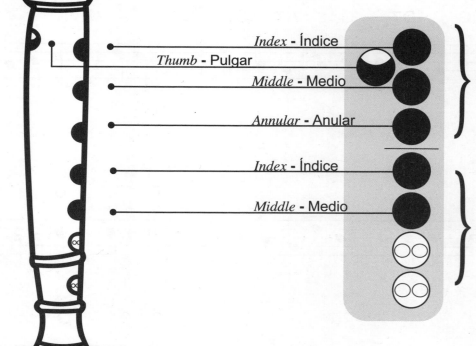

Index - Índice

Thumb - Pulgar

Middle - Medio

Annular - Anular

Index - Índice

Middle - Medio

Left Hand
Mano Izquierda

Right Hand
Mano Derecha

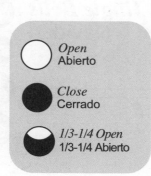

Open
Abierto

Close
Cerrado

1/3-1/4 Open
1/3-1/4 Abierto

Color the ”MI” note on the piano.
Coloree la nota “MI” en el piano.

*Every time the **Voy,** the **Blanca** or the **Marcho** is on the **Fourth Space** its name is:*
Cuando el **Voy**, la **Blanca** o el **Marcho** están en la **Espacio 4** su nombre es:

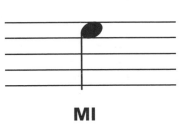

MI

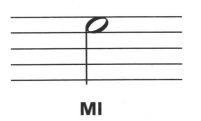

MI

MI   MI

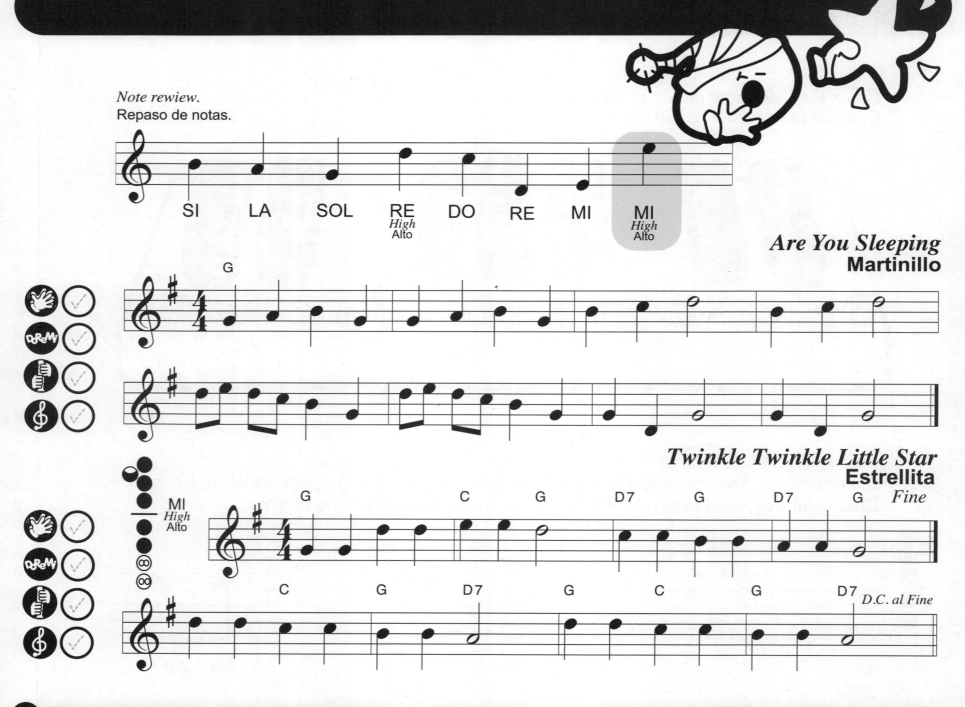

*The **FERMATA** symbol is used to hold the note or rest longer than usual.*

El símbolo de **EL CALDERÓN** se coloca sobre o bajo de cualquier nota, cuando queremos alargar una nota más tiempo del que le pertenece.

*If the **FERMATA** is like this, it goes **on top** of the note or rest.*

Si la media luna se encuentra **sobre** el punto se coloca **sobre** la nota.

*If the **FERMATA** is like this, it goes **under** the note or rest.*

Si la media luna se encuentra **bajo** el punto se coloca **bajo** la nota.

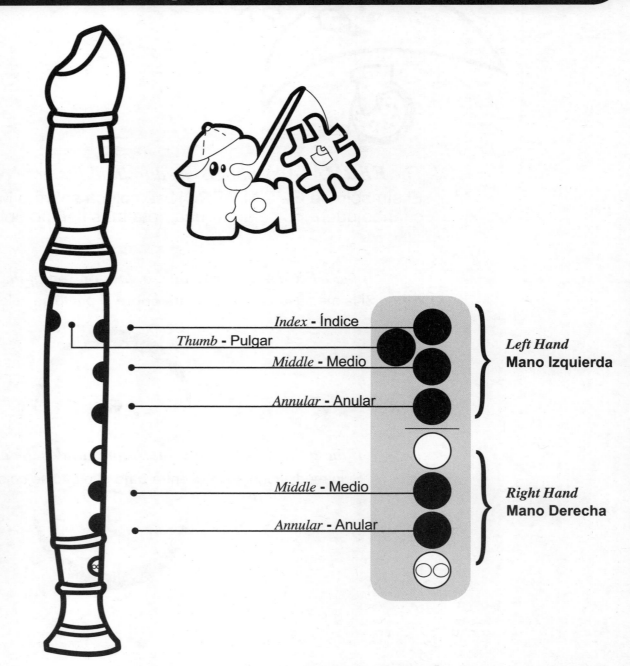

Index - Índice

Thumb - Pulgar

Middle - Medio

Annular - Anular

Left Hand
Mano Izquierda

Middle - Medio

Annular - Anular

Right Hand
Mano Derecha

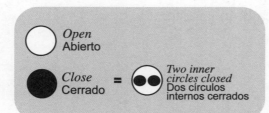

Open
Abierto

Close
Cerrado

= Two inner circles closed
Dos círculos internos cerrados

Color the"FA SHARP" note on the piano.
Coloree la nota "FA SOSTENIDO" en el piano.

*Each time there is a **Sharp** symbol on the **Fifth Line** in the beginning of the song, it means you have to play all the **Fa's Sharp.***

Cuando al comienzo de una canción se encuentra un **Sostenido** en la **Línea 5,** todas las notas que se llamen **Fa** son **Sostenidos**.

Note rewiew.
Repaso de notas.

SI   LA   SOL   RE *High Alto*   DO   RE   MI   MI *High Alto*   FA#

Happy Birthday
Feliz Cumpleaños

Good Morning Song
Las Mañanitas

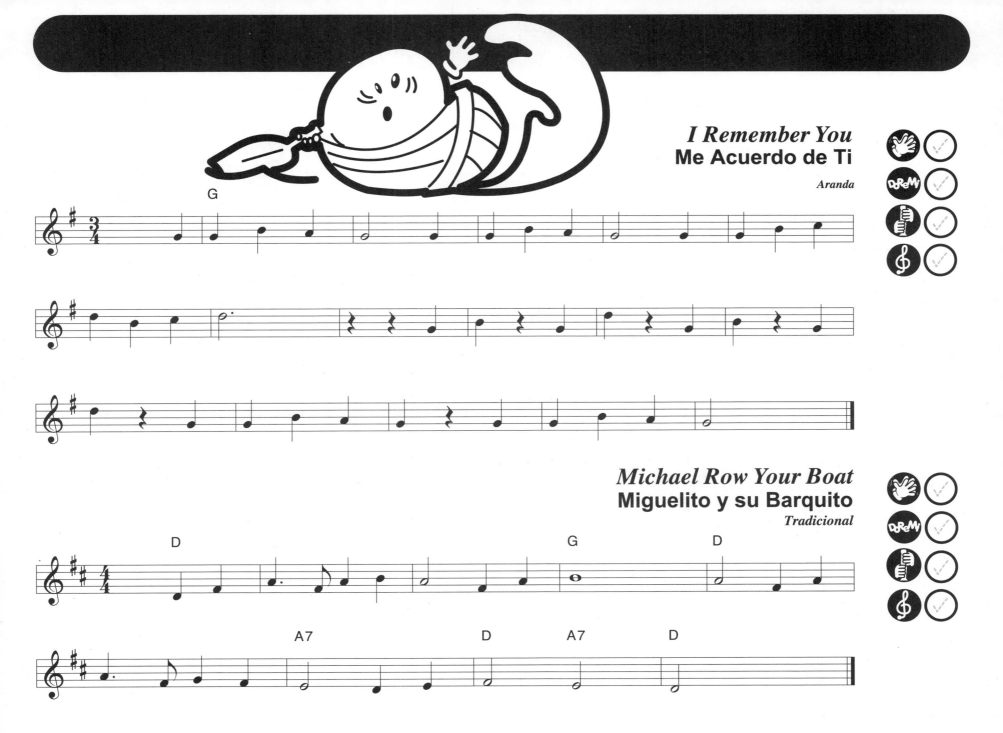

I Remember You
Me Acuerdo de Ti

Aranda

Michael Row Your Boat
Miguelito y su Barquito

Tradicional

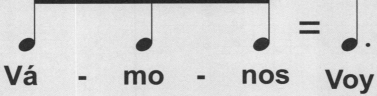

Vá - mo - nos Voy

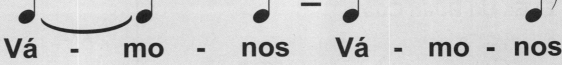

Vá - mo - nos Vá - mo - nos

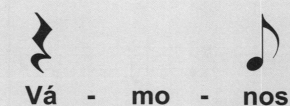

Vá - mo - nos

Voy

6

When in the beginning of a song there is a number 6 on top of a number 8 the "Voy" has a dot.

8

Cuando al comienzo de una canción está el número 6 sobre el número 8 el "Voy" lleva un punto.

My Little Ranch
Mi Ranchito

Americana

For He Is A Jolly Good Fellow
El Es Un Buen Cuate

Inglesa/Francesa

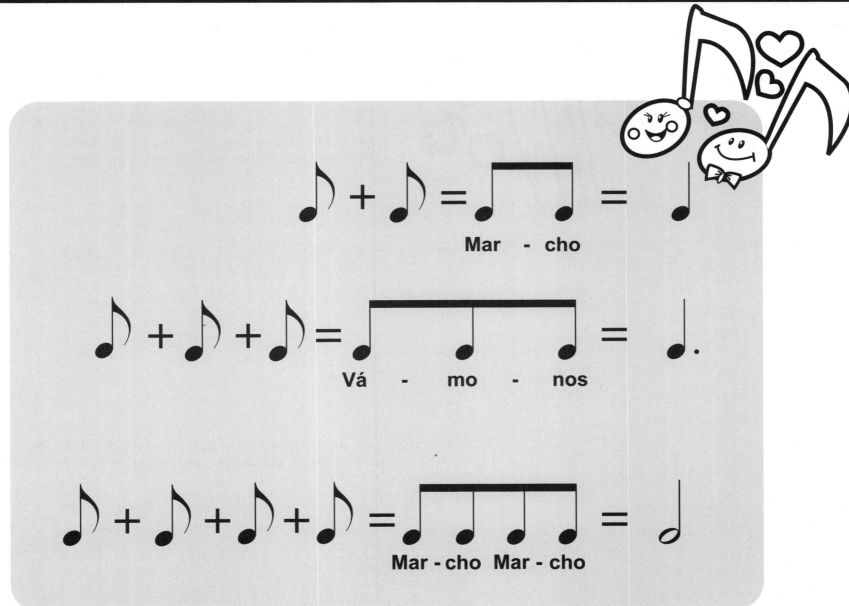

Repeat everything you see between the dots
Se repite todo lo que está entre los puntos

If there is dots only in one place, you should repeat from the beginning
Si hay puntos en un solo lugar, se repite desde el principio.

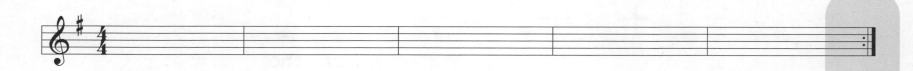

Ding Dong happiness Up High
Ding Dong Felicidad en lo Alto

Francesa

Oh Come All Ye Faithfull
Venid Fieles Todos

Inglesa

49

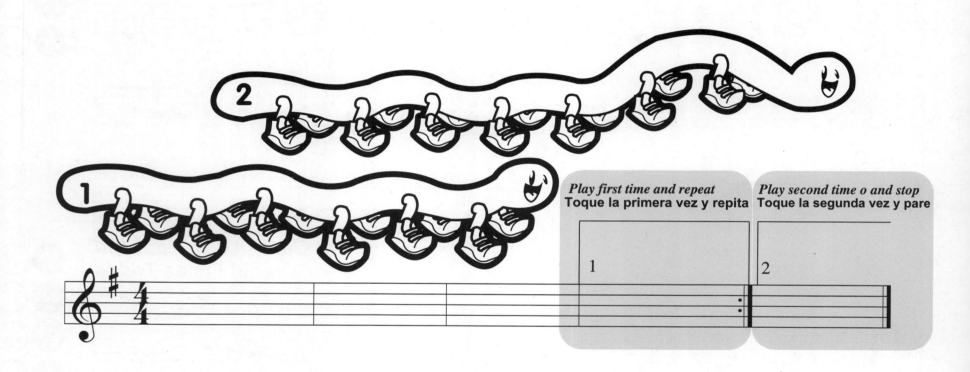

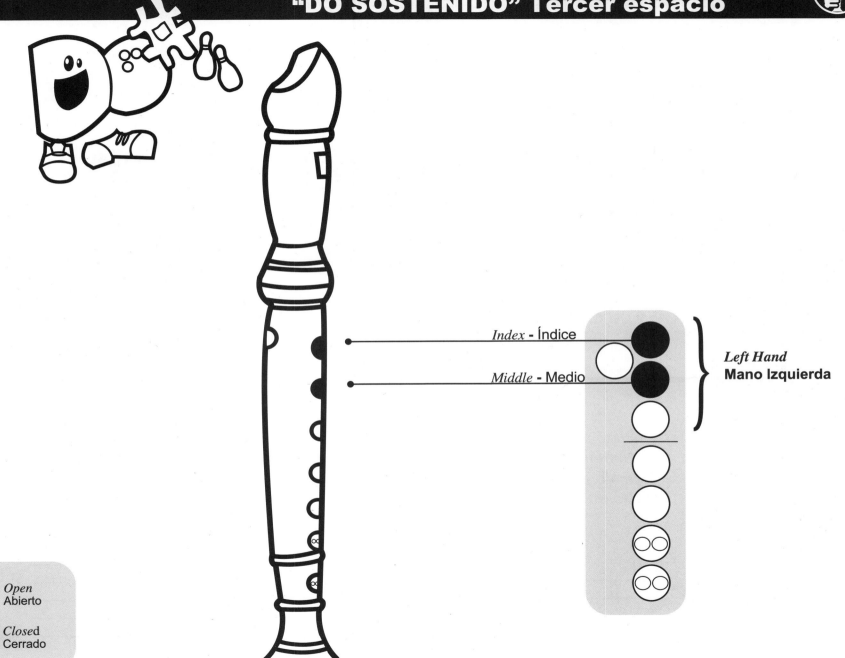

Index - Índice

Middle - Medio

Left Hand
Mano Izquierda

Open
Abierto

*Close*d
Cerrado

Color the "DO SHARP" note on the piano.
Coloree la nota "DO SOSTENIDO" en el piano.

*Each time there is a **Sharp** symbol on the **Fifth Line** & on the **Third Space** in the beginning of the song, it means you have to play all the **Fa's** and **Do's Sharp.***

Cuando al comienzo de una canción se encuentra un **Sostenido** en la **Línea 5** y otro en el **Espacio 3**, todas las notas que se llamen **Fa** y **Do** son **Sostenidos**.

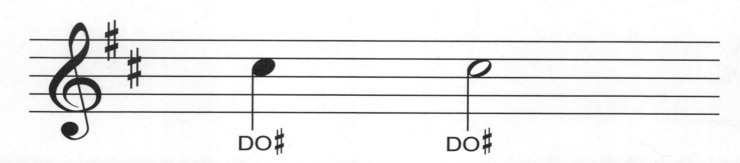

Mar - cho   Voy   Mar - cho Voy

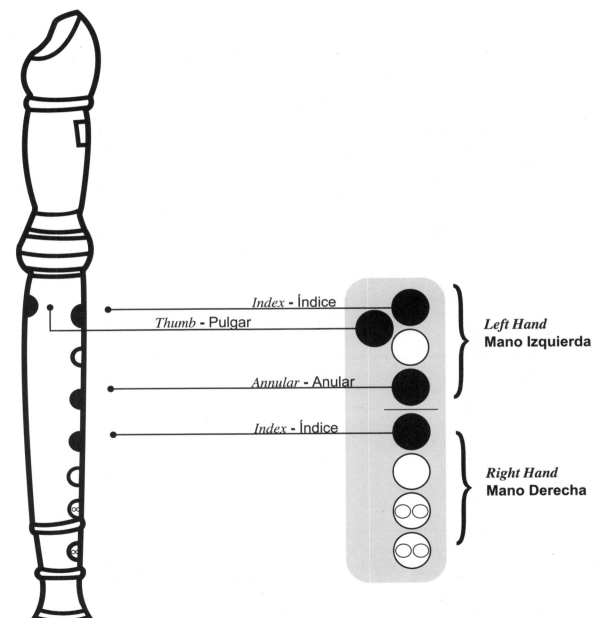

Index - Índice

Thumb - Pulgar

Left Hand
Mano Izquierda

Annular - Anular

Index - Índice

Right Hand
Mano Derecha

Open
Abierto

*Close*d
Cerrado

Color the "SI FLAT" note on the piano.
Coloree la nota "SI BEMOL" en el piano.

*Each time there is a **Flat** symbol on the **Third Line** in the beginning of the song, it means you have to play all the **Si's Flat**.*

Cuando al comienzo de una canción se encuentra un **Bemol** en la **Línea 3**, todas las notas que se llamen **Si** son **Bemol**.

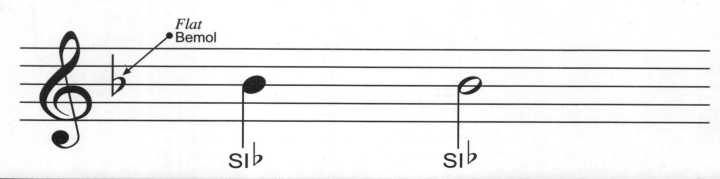

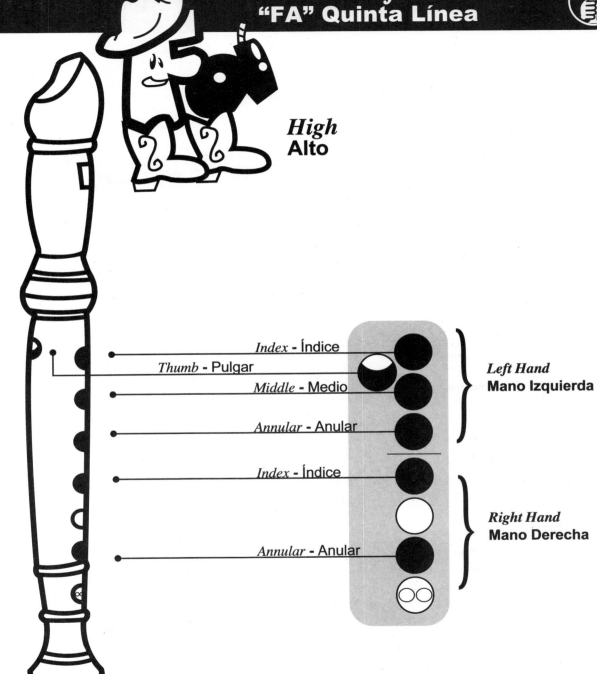

High
Alto

Index - Índice

Thumb - Pulgar

Middle - Medio

Annular - Anular

Left Hand
Mano Izquierda

Index - Índice

Right Hand
Mano Derecha

Annular - Anular

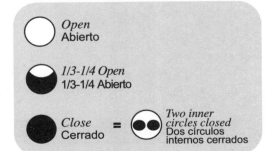

Open
Abierto

1/3-1/4 Open
1/3-1/4 Abierto

Close
Cerrado

=

Two inner circles closed
Dos círculos internos cerrados

Color the "FA" note on the piano.
Coloree la nota "FA" en el piano.

Do Re Mi Fa Sol La Si Do Re Mi Fa

Every time the Voy, the Blanca or the Marcho is on the Fifth Line its name is:
Cuando el **Voy**, la **Blanca** o el **Marcho** están en la **Línea 5** su nombre es:

FA

FA

FA   FA

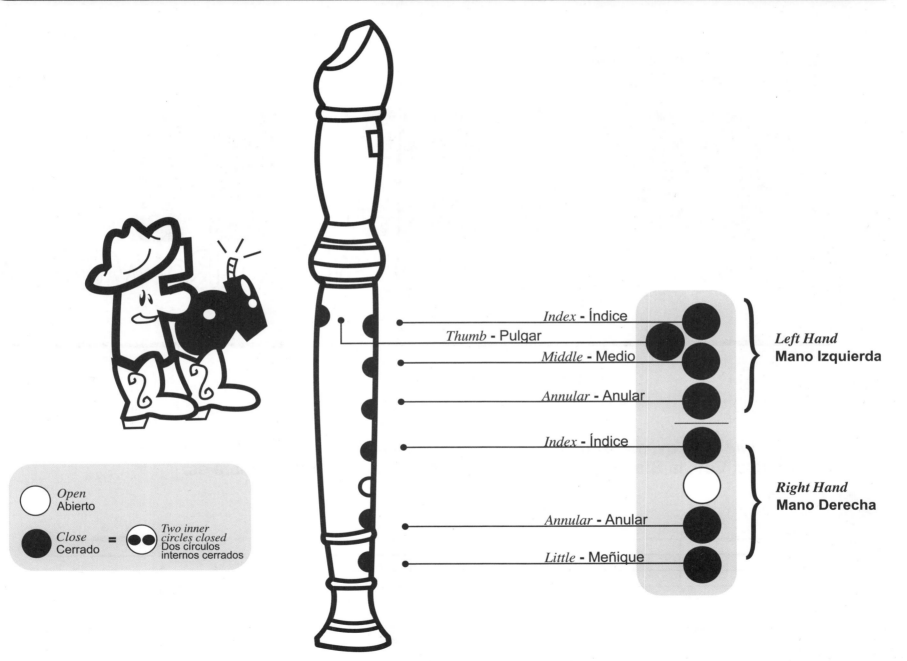

Index - Índice

Thumb - Pulgar

Middle - Medio

Annular - Anular

Left Hand
Mano Izquierda

Index - Índice

Right Hand
Mano Derecha

Annular - Anular

Little - Meñique

Open
Abierto

Close
Cerrado = Two inner circles closed
Dos círculos internos cerrados

"FA" First space
"FA" Primer espacio

Color the "FA" note on the piano.
Coloree la nota "FA" en el piano.

Do Re Mi Fa Sol La Si Do Re Mi Fa

*Every time the **Voy,** the **Blanca** or the **Marcho** is on the **First Space** its name is:*
Cuando el **Voy**, la **Blanca** o el **Marcho** están en el **Espacio 1** su nombre es:

FA

FA

FA   **FA**

Note review.
Repaso de notas.

Lullaby
Canción de Cuna

Brahms

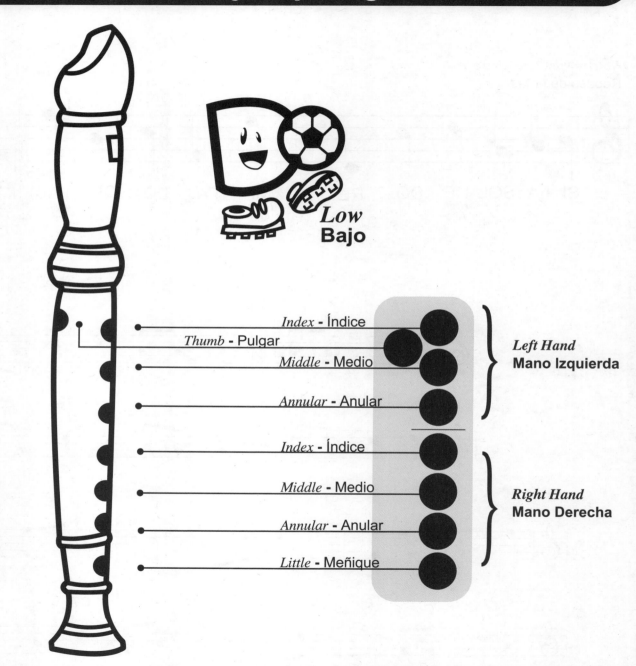

Low
Bajo

Index - Índice

Thumb - Pulgar

Middle - Medio

Annular - Anular

Left Hand
Mano Izquierda

Index - Índice

Middle - Medio

Annular - Anular

Little - Meñique

Right Hand
Mano Derecha

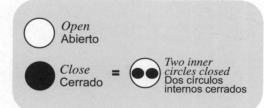

○ *Open*
Abierto

● *Close*
Cerrado

= ◖● *Two inner circles closed*
Dos círculos internos cerrados

Color the "DO" note on the piano.
Coloree la nota "DO" en el piano.

*Every time the **Voy**, the **Blanca** or the **Marcho** is on the **First Line under the staff** its name is:*
Cuando el **Voy**, la **Blanca** o el **Marcho** están en la **Primera Línea bajo el pentagrama** su nombre es:

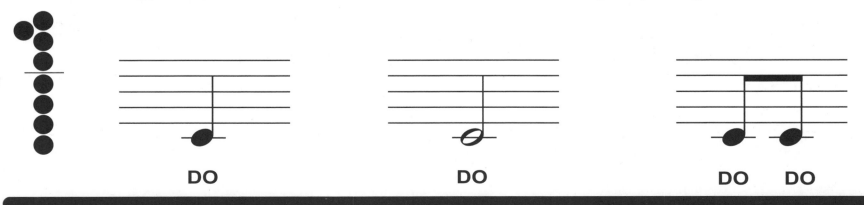

DO   DO   DO DO

*Remember all Si's are ♭'s in this song
*Recuerda que todos los Si son ♭'s en esta canción

Note rewiew.
Repaso de notas.

SI LA SOL RE *High/Alto* DO RE MI MI *High/Alto* FA♯ DO♯ SI♭ FA(♮) *High/Alto* FA(♮) DO(♮) *Low/Bajo*

From "Winter"
De "Invierno"

Vivaldi

DO *Low/Bajo*

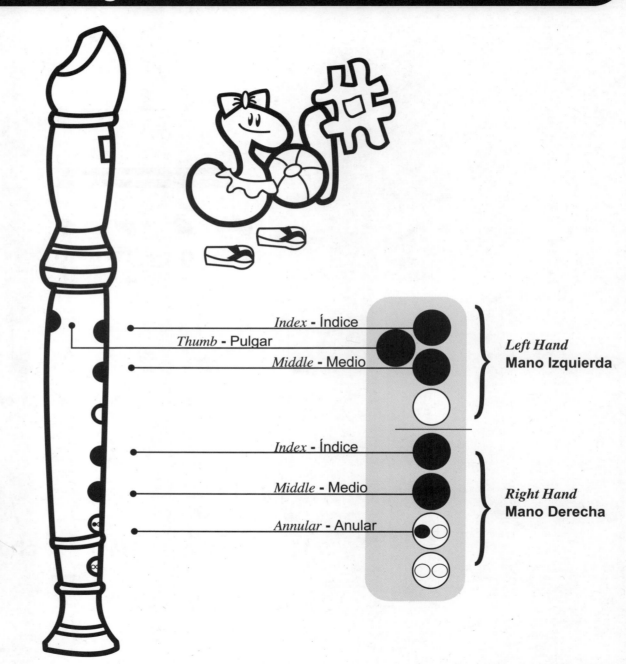

Index - Índice

Thumb - Pulgar

Middle - Medio

Left Hand
Mano Izquierda

Index - Índice

Middle - Medio

Right Hand
Mano Derecha

Annular - Anular

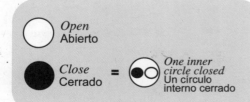

⚪ Open / Abierto	
⚫ Close / Cerrado	= ◐ One inner circle closed / Un círculo interno cerrado

Color the "SOL SHARP" note on the piano.
Coloree la nota "SOL SOSTENIDO" en el piano.

*Every time the **Voy**, the **Blanca** or the **Redondita** is on the **Second Line with a Sharp** its name is:*
Cuando el **Voy**, la **Blanca** o la **Redondit**a están en la **Línea 2 con un Sostenido** su nombre es:

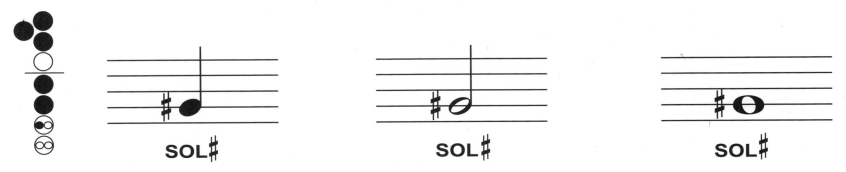

SOL♯   SOL♯   SOL♯

Note rewiew.
Repaso de notas.

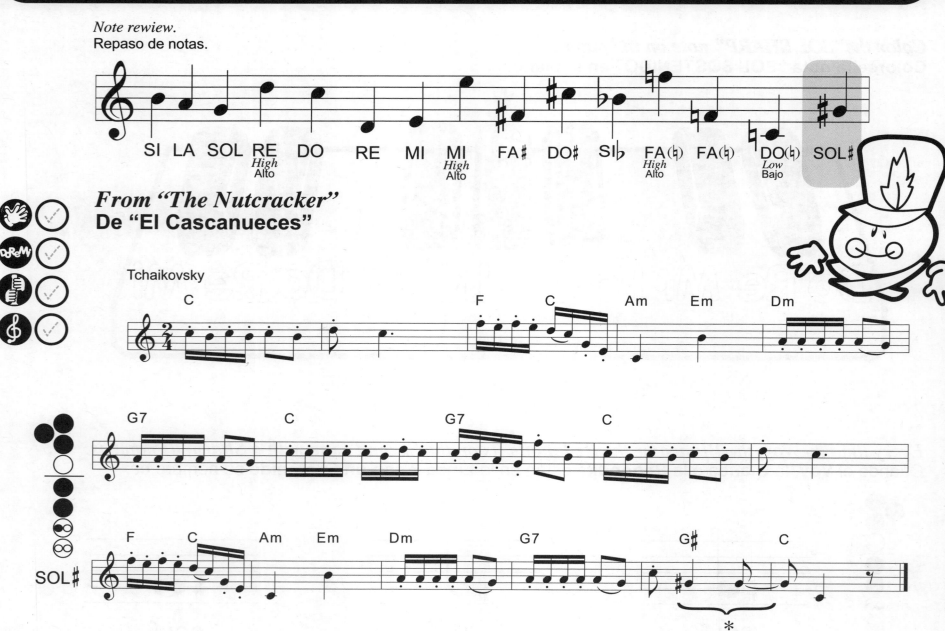

SI   LA   SOL   RE   DO   RE   MI   MI   FA#   DO#   SI♭   FA(♮)   FA(♮)   DO(♮)   SOL#
          High   *High*   *High*   *Low*
          Alto   Alto   Alto   Bajo

From "The Nutcracker"
De "El Cascanueces"

Tchaikovsky

C

F   C   Am   Em   Dm

G7   C   G7   C

F   C   Am   Em   Dm   G7   G#   C

SOL#

*

68

Sailor
Marinero

Inglesa

Beautiful Heaven
Cielito Lindo

Mexicana

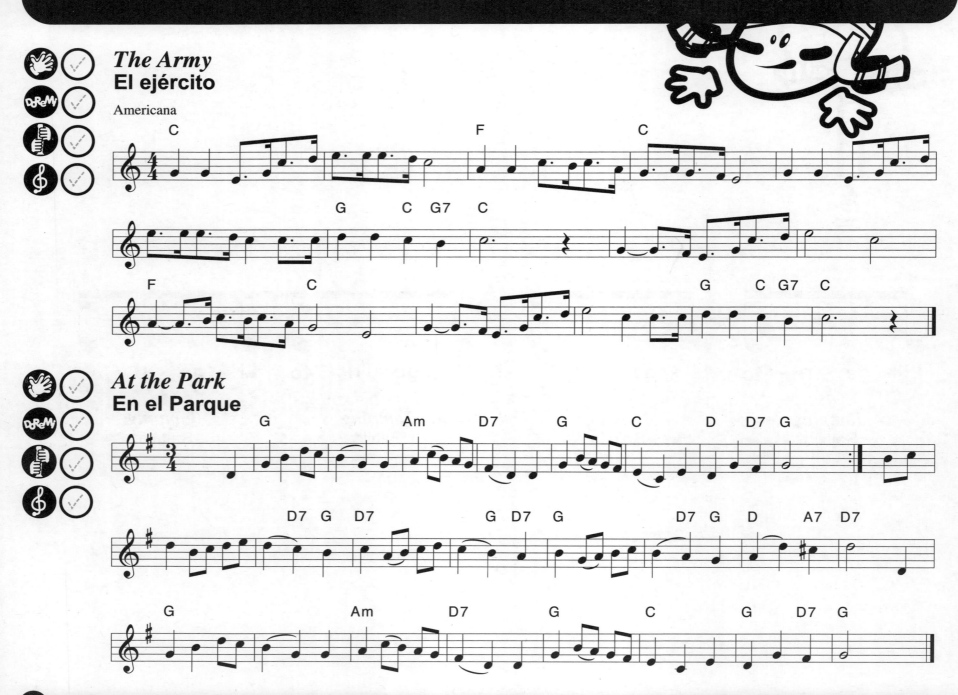

The Army
El ejército

At the Park
En el Parque

New Year
Año Nuevo

The Fair
En la Feria

Inglesa

Silent Night
Noche de Paz

Gruber

The First Noel
El Primer Noel

Tradicional

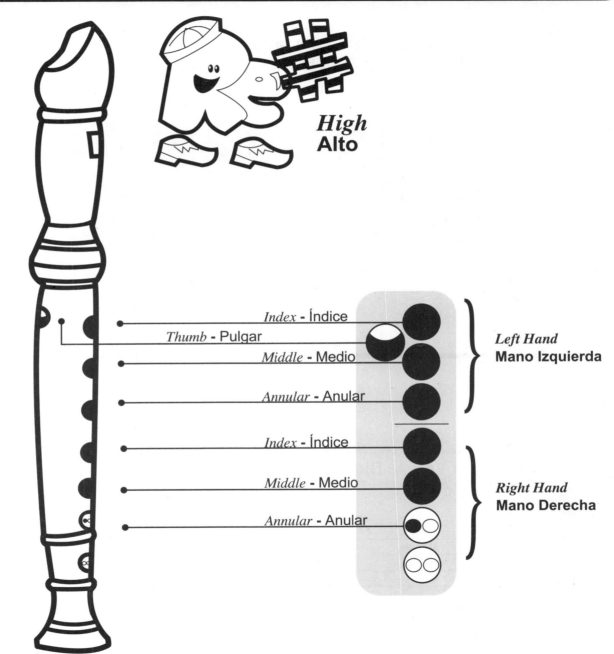

High
Alto

Index - Índice

Thumb - Pulgar

Middle - Medio

Left Hand
Mano Izquierda

Annular - Anular

Index - Índice

Middle - Medio

Right Hand
Mano Derecha

Annular - Anular

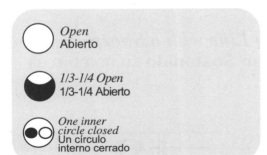

Open
Abierto

1/3-1/4 Open
1/3-1/4 Abierto

One inner circle closed
Un círculo interno cerrado

Color the "RE SHARP" note on the piano.
Coloree la nota "RE SOSTENIDO" en el piano.

*Every time the **Voy**, the **Blanca** or the **Redondita** is on the **Fourth Line with a Sharp** its name is:*
Cuando el **Voy**, la **Blanca** o la **Redondit**a están en la **Línea 4 con un Sostenido** su nombre es:

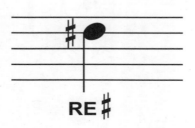

RE ♯

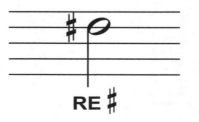

RE ♯

RE ♯

From "Serenade"
De "Serenata"
Haydn

From "Swan Lake"
De "El Lago de los Cisnes"
Tchaikovsky

RE
High
Alto

77

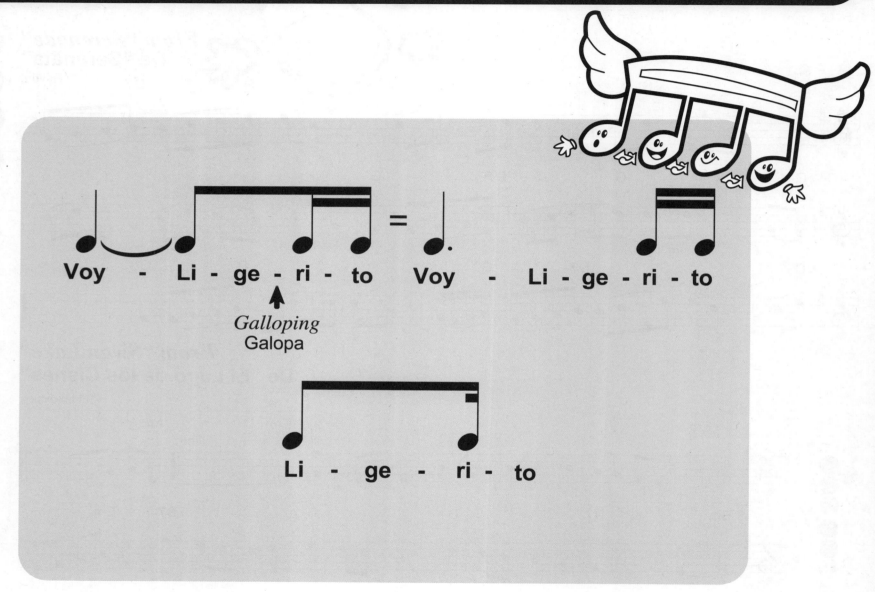

Voy - Li - ge - ri - to Voy - Li - ge - ri - to

Galloping
Galopa

Li - ge - ri - to

From "Spring"
De "Primavera"

Vivaldi

Romance
Romance

Mozart

The Holly and the Ivy
El Acebo y la Hiedra

Tradicional

The Good Morning Song
Las Mañanitas

Mexicana

First Lesson
Primera Lección

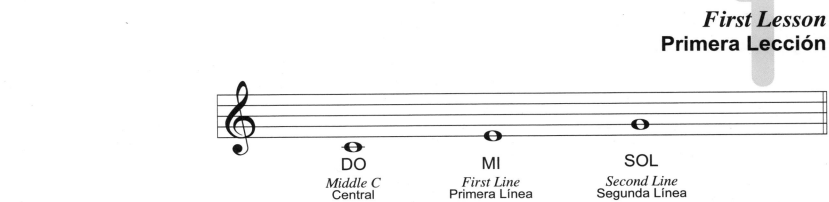

DO
Middle C
Central

MI
First Line
Primera Línea

SOL
Second Line
Segunda Línea

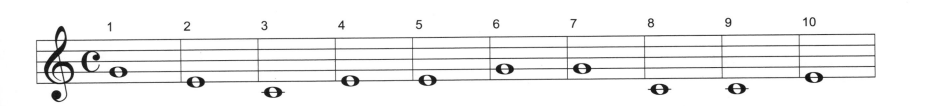

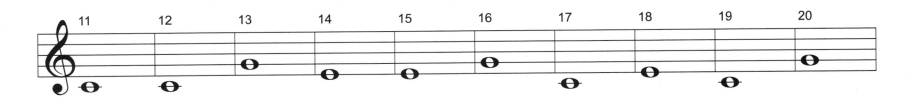

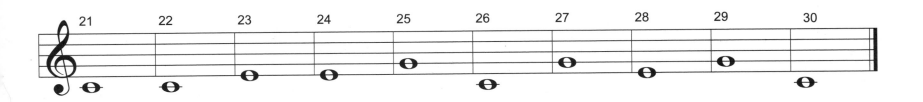

Second Lesson
Segunda Lección

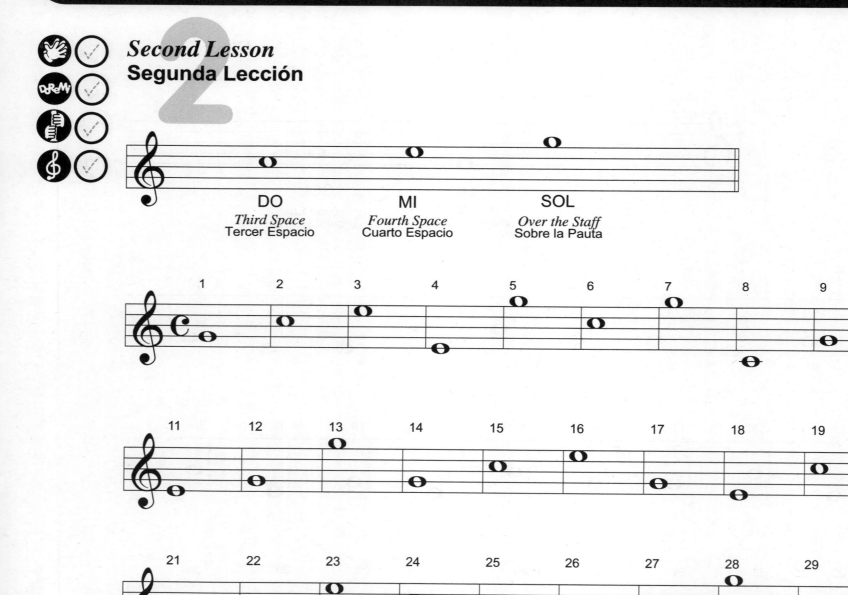

DO
Third Space
Tercer Espacio

MI
Fourth Space
Cuarto Espacio

SOL
Over the Staff
Sobre la Pauta

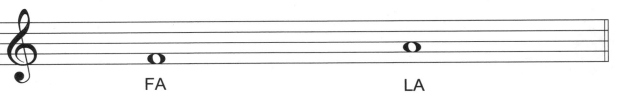

FA

First Space
Primer Espacio

LA

Second Space
Segundo Espacio

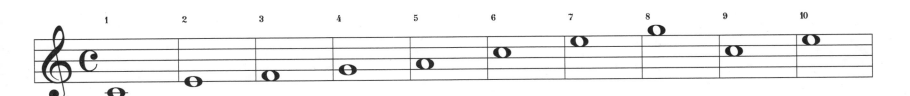

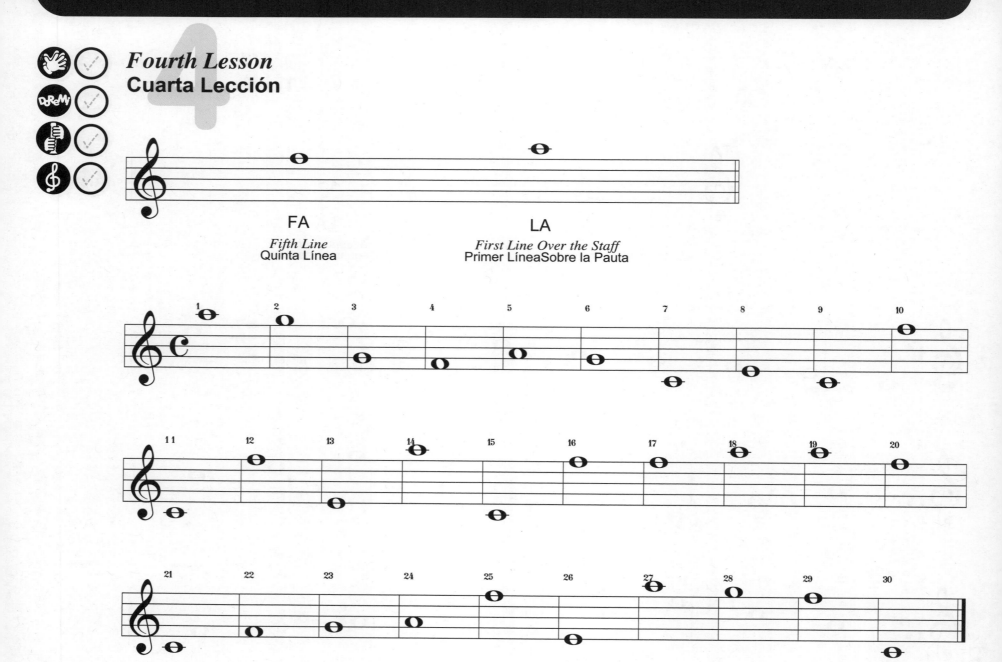

Fourth Lesson
Cuarta Lección

FA
Fifth Line
Quinta Línea

LA
First Line Over the Staff
Primer LíneaSobre la Pauta

Fifth Lesson
Quinta Lección

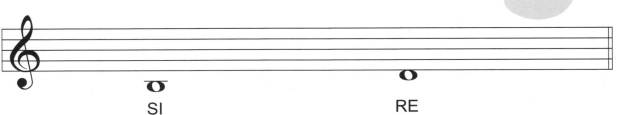

SI
Under the First Line Under the Staff
Bajo la Primer Línea Adicional

RE
Under the Staff
Bajo el Pentagrama

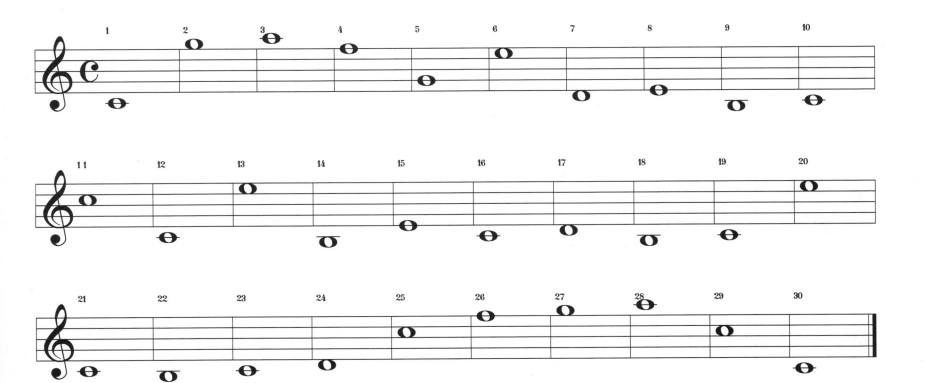

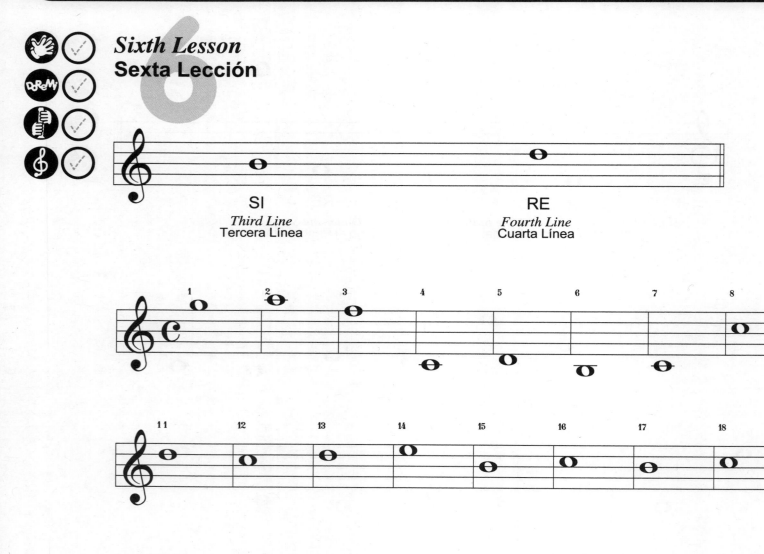

SI
Third Line
Tercera Línea

RE
Fourth Line
Cuarta Línea

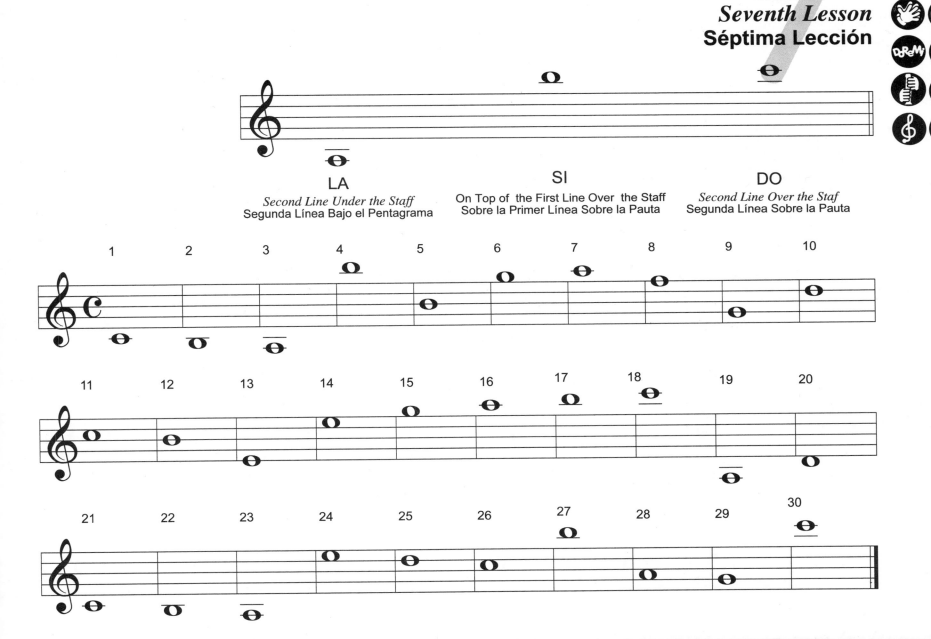

LA
Second Line Under the Staff
Segunda Línea Bajo el Pentagrama

SI
On Top of the First Line Over the Staff
Sobre la Primer Línea Sobre la Pauta

DO
Second Line Over the Staf
Segunda Línea Sobre la Pauta

Low Range
Registro Bajo

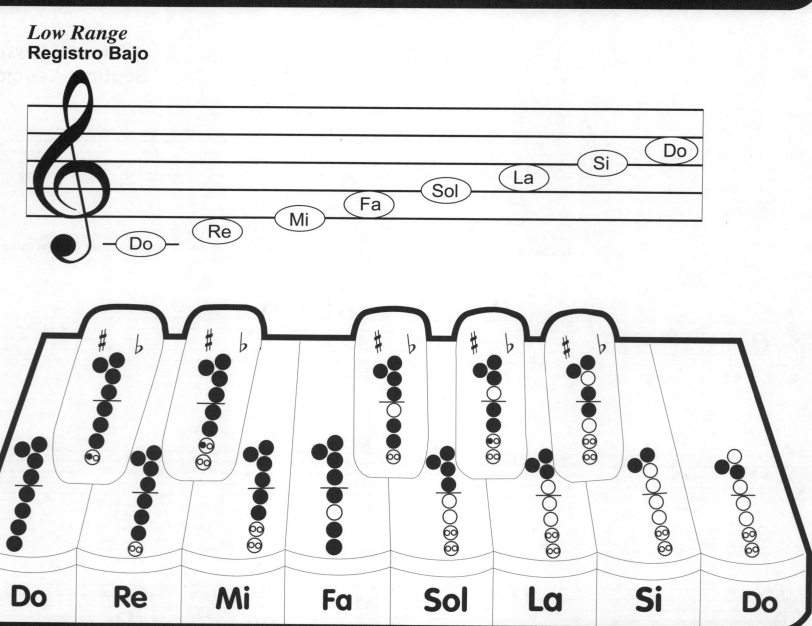

High Range
Registro Alto

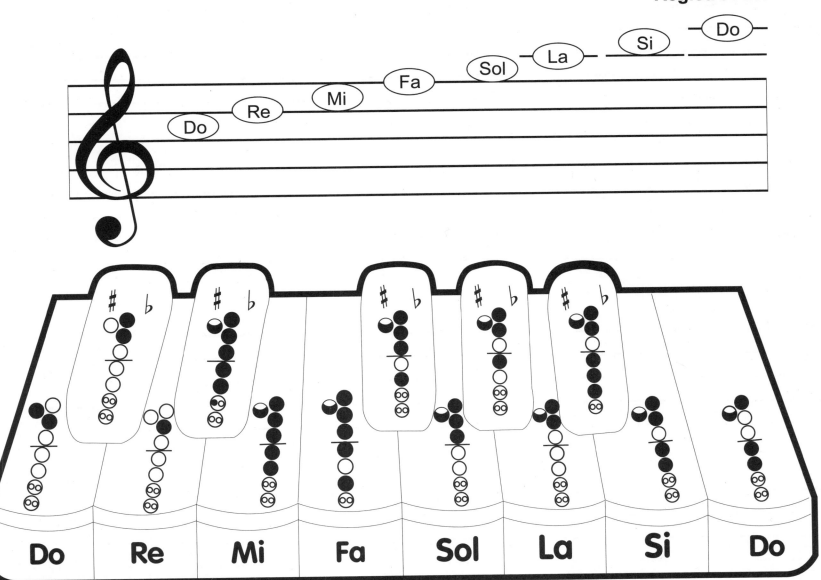

Staff Paper
Papel Pautado

Escuela de Música

Certificate of Achievement
Certificado de Mérito

This certifies that:
Certifica que:

Name
Nombre _____

has succesfully completed "Mi Pri.mer Libro de Música" and is now ready to begin next lever or instrument book.

ha terminado exitosamente "MI PRIMER LIBRO DE MÚSICA" y ahora está listo para empezar el siguiente nivel o libro de instrumento.

Date
Fecha _____

Teacher
Maestro _____